VIOLIN
Techniqu
in practice

Daily exercises to maintain and improve violin technique

MARY COHEN

FABER *ff* MUSIC

© 2020 by Faber Music Ltd
This edition first published in 2020 by Faber Music Ltd
Bloomsbury House
74–77 Great Russell Street
London WC1B 3DA

Music processed by Donald Thomson
Cover and concept design by Susan Clarke
Cover image: Alexkava (Getty Images)
Page design and illustrations by Elizabeth Ogden
Printed in England by Caligraving Ltd

ISBN10: 0-571-54157-7
EAN13: 978-0-571-54157-7

To buy Faber Music publications or to find out about the full range of titles available
please contact your local music retailer or Faber Music sales enquiries:

Faber Music Limited, Burnt Mill, Elizabeth Way, Harlow, CM20 2HX England
Tel: +44 (0) 1279 82 89 82 Fax: +44 (0) 1279 82 89 83
sales@fabermusic.com   fabermusicstore.com

Contents

Introduction

Complex music is constructed from thousands of moments of simplicity. What creates the complexity is these moments evolving and linking, in a series of transitions.

I've spent my musical life noticing the essence of things. Simplifying technique and eliminating the unnecessary, but always with 'the music' as my aim.

Technique in practice is a compilation of short exercises that I've improvised and jotted down over decades, now collated into ten progressive sets. It's material that I use for myself, to keep (or return) my playing to performance standard. And I also use it appropriately with my pupils, of all ages.

There's a myth that for violinists the absolute priority is to be able to play incredibly high, fast, and with great vibrato. Yes, to do these things well is important, and very satisfying to achieve. But countless times I have encountered players who, by concentrating on these things alone, find it hardest to play well in the lower positions, or slowly, or without vibrato.

We can (unconsciously) be working at a tempo too fast for us to hear our problems. But someone listening – even a non-player – might sense the inaccuracies that we are choosing not to listen to and find this an uncomfortable experience. Many of the exercises in this book offer a range of metronome marks. The slowest is often the hardest and most revealing option – but be brave and tackle it. (You may want to try an even slower tempo than the metronome marks!)

To play accurately in high positions, we need good foundations in the lower positions. And it's in those lower positions that we experience the most rotation and arm extension. In performance, we need to be adjusting the rotation, the elbow position, and hand height, as necessary, on autopilot. So, over the course of the whole book, there are exercises designed to develop confident familiarity with every part of the instrument. (And if you want to extend some of the E string material and go higher, it should be obvious how to continue a sequence with extra bars.)

If we want to be able to play 'authentically' in styles from the 1600s to the present day, we need to be able to switch between a variety of vibrato types and bowing strokes. Being able to turn vibrato on and off, use it 'lightly', or with discretion, is an essential part of a modern player's technique. And practising without vibrato is not just important for 'revealing' intonation, it's also important when working at tone production with the bow.

Getting the instrument out of the case for personal practice can sometimes feel like an effort, so this book is designed to give you a friendly 'companion', talking you through the exercises like a personal trainer.

Always remember to LISTEN, THINK and ENJOY!

Mary Cohen

How to use this book

Technique in practice is a resource to explore and use in a way that suits your own playing and situation at any given time. Personally, I use the sets as warm-ups, as a time to think in depth about technique, and sometimes to give my technique a deep clean. When it's possible, I play the sets through as a cycle, one a day over a couple of weeks or so, allowing for an occasional day off! For intermediate players the first few sets are a good starting point, and for advanced adult pupils or professional players, I suggest starting by repeating each set a few times, to feel the flow of ideas and the gradual increase in level of difficulty. Use this book in the way that seems most helpful to you and make use of the blank pages to note your own ideas.

Which string to use

I = E string

II = A string

III = D string

IV = G string

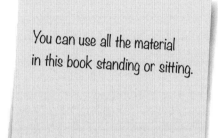

You can use all the material in this book standing or sitting.

Sul E (or Sul A, Sul D, Sul G) = use only that string throughout

Follow the fingerings

The printed fingerings are key to the essence of the techniques covered in each exercise.

Metronome marks

Where metronome marks are indicated, a 'c.' before the number indicates some flexibility of tempo either way. A dash between the numbers indicates a wide range of options from slow to fast.

Time and key signatures

I've adopted the convention of no time signatures for the exercises but have used time signatures for the Tech-Synthesis pieces and for the sequence of bowing variations on pages 54-55. Equally, open key signatures are used where more useful and appropriate.

The Golden Tone exercises

All 10 sets in this book start with a Golden Tone Exercise. The basic version of this was passed on to me by Roger Best and I've since created several variants. These exercises help players to develop and maintain control everywhere in the bow – and also open up the sound of the instrument.

My essential one-minute pre-practising preparation

❖ **A quick *pp* pizzicato check to hear if strings are in tune**

If they are reasonably in tune, I *deliberately* don't do any tuning at this stage. (The moment of tuning with the bow is part of the warming up process, coming soon!)

❖ **Zoning into weightless balance (without instrument or bow)**

Before picking up the violin or bow, I begin by going into a state of 'weightless balance' which I teach to colleagues and pupils like this:

Imagine standing in a warm sea, on a flat sandy bank, with feet apart and knees slightly bent. Adapt this idea appropriately if you are sitting.

The water is about chest-high, so your arms and hands are able to float weightlessly at the surface, palms facing downwards. Let your elbows find a natural position, slightly lower than your hands, and think of a 'line' (as dancers say) along the forearms, past the wrist, right to the knuckles.

The salty sea is supporting your arms, which rise and fall a little as you breathe. Your knees are flexible and slightly bent, so the pull of the tide is rocking you gently, almost diagonally, from side to side, in balanced weightlessness. (If you are sitting, you can still imagine the diagonal sideways pull of the tide rocking you.) Keep this sensation of weightless balance in your mind, as you raise your arms from the imaginary sea and begin to play long bows on an 'air violin'!

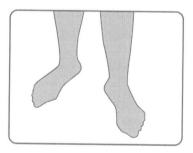

Foot position: standing

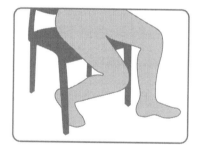

Foot position: sitting

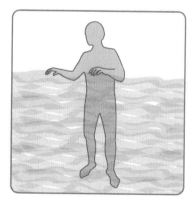

Weightless balance

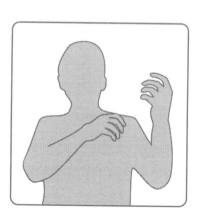

Air violin

If you are not yet feeling the weightlessness, take a break, then try imagining the scene again. It may take a few sessions to completely 'get' this feeling but it's like all skills which require balance – once you have acquired the balance, it is always there for you to zone back into. Once you've learned how to do this, going into weightless balance can be done instantaneously!

❖ Almost silent 'lifting and landing' (with instrument and bow)

Standing or seated, find a balanced weightless posture. Breathing calmly, place the violin so it's very comfortable and keep the left hand relaxed, fingers above the strings, in around third or fourth position.

With a comfortable bow hold, land the bow silently, flat on the A string, right at the heel. Stay still, and memorise the sensation of this bow hold, at the heel. Notice how the fingers and thumb feel, and how both the upper arm and elbow relate to the body.

Lift the bow, land it in the middle of the string. Now play a quiet note, with flat hair, which takes you from the middle right to the point. Stay motionless at the point for a moment and memorise how the fingers and thumb feel now, and where the upper arm and elbow are in relation to the body.

Lift the bow and begin a sequence of almost silent 'lifting and landing', first at the heel, then at the point, and so on, repeating this for about 30 seconds.

Landing silently at the heel is straightforward but it's much harder at the point. If the bow bounces when landing at the point, there is some tension in the fingers and hand – reducing the 'grip' of the bow hold to an absolute minimum should cushion the landings.

> **An extra thought:** *If you are finding it difficult (or even physically impossible) to keep your little finger on the stick when at the point, try adjusting the relationship between your arms and the centre of your body. If this doesn't work, consider trying a shorter bow. Following a major accident several decades ago, I switched to a $^3/_4$ size bow 'just to get back to playing'. I've got short arms and found using a $^3/_4$ size bow made a huge difference to how easy and comfortable it felt 'landing' at the point; I never did go back to a full-size bow, and no one ever noticed...*

Making the most of our brains when practising

How does the brain take on board information when we are playing? If you think of yourself and your instrument as one unit, what the brain is doing is taking millions and millions of super quick measurements about this unit, in 3-dimensional space.

Receptors send a message to the brain, to record the length of individual muscles, tendons, and ligaments at any given moment. In co-ordination with our ears and sensory system, what is being put together is in effect a massive physical encyclopaedia. This constantly updated encyclopaedia knows where everything needs to be in 3-D space, for our 'person + instrument' unit to recreate our playing. We are developing what's called proprioception.

However, the brain doesn't distinguish between what is good for our playing and what isn't. If we practise the same faults over and over, that faulty way will become the brain's default route. But we players can take control by stopping, thinking, and learning from our mistakes. This intervention can help the brain to create new, more appropriate pathways.

The brain acquires information by firing electrical impulses, some of which bump into each other, forming useful temporary links. But to turn these into long-term retrievable memories, the brain needs time to produce a chemical to coat and permanently bond the links.

Amazingly, violin teachers have known for over two centuries that it's best to practise technique in tiny sections, taking little breaks. We've probably all heard the instruction, "Play for a bar-and-a-note then stop. Play for another bar-and-a-note then stop." Now science has given us an explanation for why this works. During rest, the brain can consolidate what it has recently acquired and transfer memories from temporary to permanent storage. So we should learn to pace our practising sessions, and to give the brain the time it needs to function properly.

In addition, it can be useful to spend time practising 'in the mind' (away from the instrument and music page), running through what has resulted in positive improvements and good auto-pathways.

Learning to analyse in a calm and neutral way helps all of our practising. The crucial thing is to avoid being negative or self-critical. A healthy way to think is to ask yourself, *"What could I try instead?"*

Set 1

This set is a good starting point for establishing and re-establishing a regular practice routine, ideal for intermediate students or returning players. Technique and 'the music' are inextricably linked companions. While trying to keep technique clean when practising, never let it become robotic.

❖   Introducing the Golden Tone exercise

❖   Left-hand finger accuracy and flexibility

❖   String crossings

❖   Left-hand freedom in glissando techniques

❖   Shifting

❖   Tech-Synthesis 1

I use the ten sets in this book as a cycle. When I return to Set 1, I wonder what I'll notice about my playing this time...

Preparation for Golden Tone exercise 1

❖ Before picking up the violin and bow, think of a tempo at around ♩ = 54 for a few beats. This is going to be the 'heartbeat' for the exercise.

❖ Standing or seated, find a balanced, weightless posture. Breathing calmly, place the violin so it's very comfortable, and keep the left hand relaxed, fingers above the strings, in around third or fourth position.

❖ Place the bow at the heel on the A string, right by the bridge (with no gap), staying motionless for a moment, 'feeling the line' from the knuckles, through the wrist to the elbow.

❖ When everything is balanced, allow the body weight to continually transfer from one leg to the other during the course of four beats. (You can still do some weight transfer when seated.) Now you're ready for the exercise itself...

The exercise

❖ This is simply two very, very, slow whole bows! With the bow at the heel, feel for a balance in the centre of the right hand, then start to play right by the bridge, with flat hair throughout.

❖ Following the curve of the stick, as the bow moves towards the point, feel that the balance transfers naturally from the middle of the hand to the first finger, then back to the middle of the hand as it returns to the heel.

❖ Without pressing or gripping in any way, let your balanced arm weight feel, and maintain, an intense contact between the hair and the string.

❖ Okay, in this extremely slow tempo, this doesn't sound at all 'golden' to the ear, and it's hard to keep the movement fluent! So don't focus on the sound – what's more important is that you feel constant movement in the bow and that your right arm and right-hand fingers adjust as the bow moves, millimetre by millimetre.

If you keep the little finger 'just resting' weightlessly on the stick, the hand and arm will naturally rise slightly during the ⊓, and fall slightly during the Ⅴ.

Golden Tone 1

Stay calm and balanced – and don't worry about how strange this sounds!

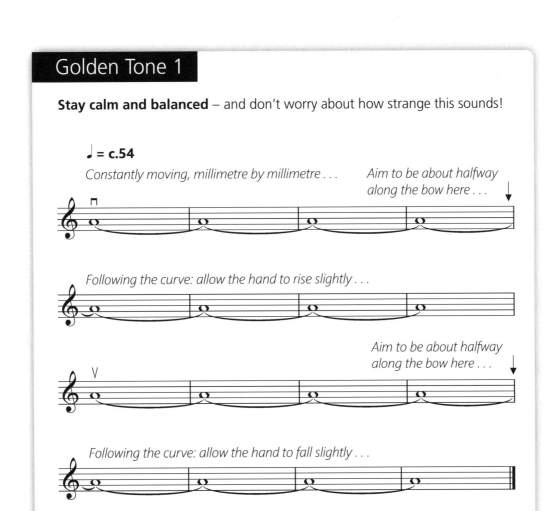

 Now tune violin, as normal

While playing all the Golden Tone exercises, really go into the zone, imagining the journey that the sound waves make inside the violin, travelling into all the corners, activating the whole instrument.

Left-hand finger accuracy and flexibility 1 The unusual order of the strings
is specifically aimed at developing left arm and elbow adjustment. On each string,
move your elbow to the position where all the fingers can drop equally easily onto
the fingerboard. The downward finger action should have just enough energy to
make and keep good contact against the fingerboard, and fingers should lift upwards
'actively' too, with a light, springy feeling. I like to keep fingers down where possible,
but you can try both ways.

String crossings While listening to the intonation, check the angle of the fingers,
so the pads don't catch the upper string, and listen for the balance of the 'tune line'
against the open strings too. Again, I like to keep fingers down where possible.

Slurred string crossings Try to use as little right arm movement and bow travel as necessary. In the repeats, check visually that the angle between the hair and the string is just enough to move from one string to the other and no wider. Keep fingers down where possible.

♩ = 116-138

1. ⊓
2. V

Silent, and almost silent, glissando 'polishing exercises' (without the bow): In first position, let the left-hand thumb and the side of the base of the first finger feel a harmonic-like contact against the neck, keeping the fingertips clear of the strings. Firstly, do some silent fast 'polishing' up and down the neck, just to the shoulder of the instrument and back. Then let the fingertips join in, polishing with the lightest of harmonic pressure on the strings – almost silently.

Glissando in harmonics Start in weightless balance. To keep this weightless feeling, try this: when the left hand is moving towards the bridge, imagine it's gliding very slightly downhill, towards the level of your chin. Then, when it's moving back towards first position, imagine the left hand gliding very slightly uphill, to about the level of your nose.

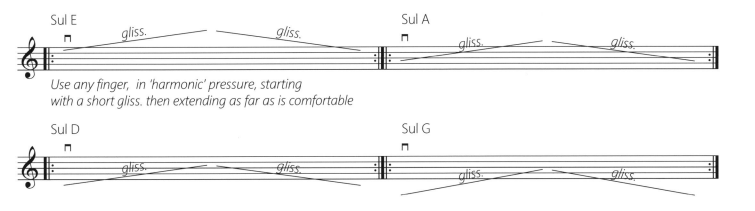

Use any finger, in 'harmonic' pressure, starting
with a short gliss. then extending as far as is comfortable

Simple shifts With only one finger on the string at a time, play cleanly, listening to the melody line of the top notes. Take a moment for your brain to process each section before starting the next one.

Slurred string crossing and double stopping Listen for the top notes as a melody line, balancing the bow arm weight slightly towards the higher string. With just the right amount of bow travel and energy, double stopping can resonate so much there's no need for vibrato. Try playing the repeat faster, and this time add some vibrato where it feels appropriate.

♩ = 96-120

1. At a moderate tempo, non vib.
2. Conjuring up a lively style

Shifts with varied fingerings In this surprisingly tricky exercise, listen for the top notes being in tune and sounding exactly the same each time. Each fingering needs some adjustment of the left elbow and left hand positions. The descending shifts use light, linked staccato notes.

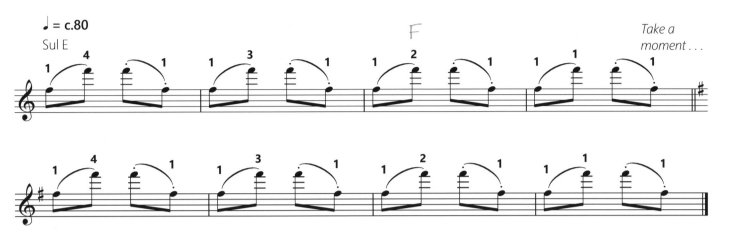

Tech-Synthesis 1

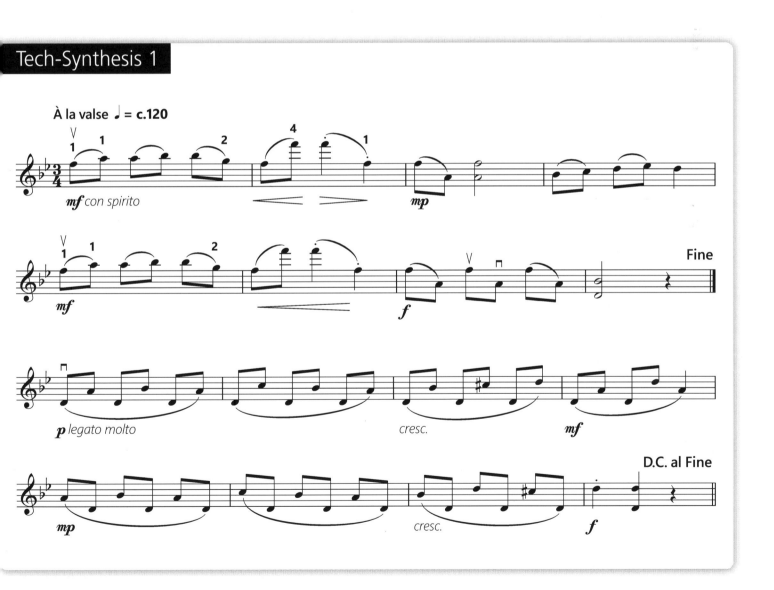

Notes

Set 2

The creaky Golden Tone exercise in this set helps to maintain a good 90° relationship between the bow and the string – a great ingredient for working at tone production. And in this extremely slow tempo the brain collects huge amounts of data. In complete contrast, enjoy a feeling of freedom in the string crossings, sequences and double stopping in the rest of the set.

- ❖ Golden Tone 2: in creaky slow motion

- ❖ Developing left-hand finger accuracy and flexibility

- ❖ Developing string crossings, with bowing variety

- ❖ Double stopping in sixths

- ❖ Contracting the hand in ascending patterns

- ❖ Tech-Synthesis 2

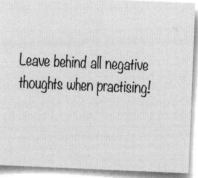

Leave behind all negative thoughts when practising!

Golden Tone 2

Ultimate 'creaky' version of the Golden Tone exercise Right by the bridge, without gripping the bow, maintain an extremely intense contact between bow hair and string, using a tempo that's slow enough to produce just a lot of 'creaks'. This exercise enables you to feel the right hand and fingers adapting, when using the full extent of the bow in both directions. Don't try to make a continuous sound, the little gaps between creaks are an essential part of the exercise. As well as helping to develop ergonomic bowing that has no unnecessary or exaggerated movements, it's a great special effect to amuse young audiences or little pupils!

Think: horribly creaky — as if pushing open a stiff wooden door! Use flat hair throughout and take as long as you like.

Now tune violin, as normal

Left-hand finger accuracy and flexibility 2 Another warm-up exercise, with different combinations of tones and semitones. This time the slurs of different lengths add an element of phrasing and bow control. For variety add some dynamics, choose from the range of tempi, and sometimes start V.

String crossings over 2 strings, with bowing variety You never know when
someone (perhaps a non-string-playing conductor...) will ask you to play a passage like
this starting with an ⋁ rather than a ⊓ , so this exercise develops fluency in both ways.
Sometimes slur 2, 6, or 12 notes to a bow, and alternate which string you do this on.
In passages like this, always be aware of the left-hand finger angles, making sure the
pads don't catch on the open string.

♩ = 116-144

1. Separate bows, starting ⊓
2. Separate bows, starting ⋁
3. With slurs

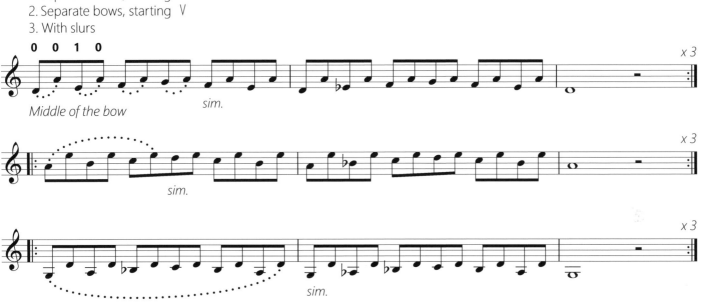

Separate or slurred string crossings in triplets It's exhilarating to play this fast,
but start with slow practice, listening carefully for evenness of notes and good intonation.
For more variety, try the slurring options on different strings.

♩. = 92-126

1. Separate bows, starting ⊓
2. With slurs

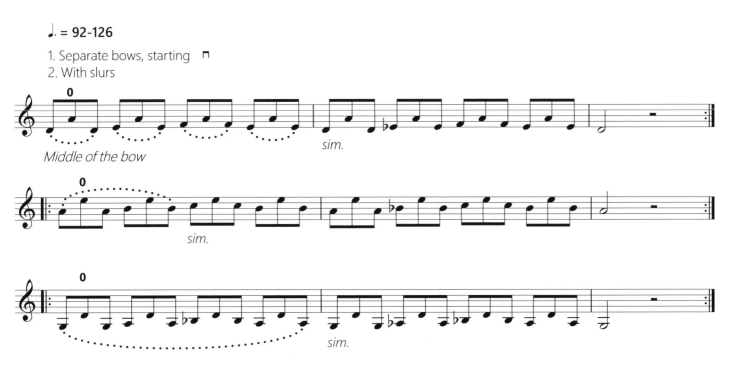

Major and minor sixths In this sequence of sixths, listen for the rising pattern of wide 'chromatic' semitones, as in 'tempered tuning'. As sixths are used so much in both Baroque and Romantic music, it's interesting and useful to try this exercise first without vibrato, then with vibrato.

♩ = c.108

Take a moment . . .

Splitting three-part and four-part chords into 2 + 2 When working at chords, start by checking that the bow is at 90° to the string. As you would in a piece, aim for a melodic line in the top notes, 'leaning' a little more on the upper strings.

♩ = c.104

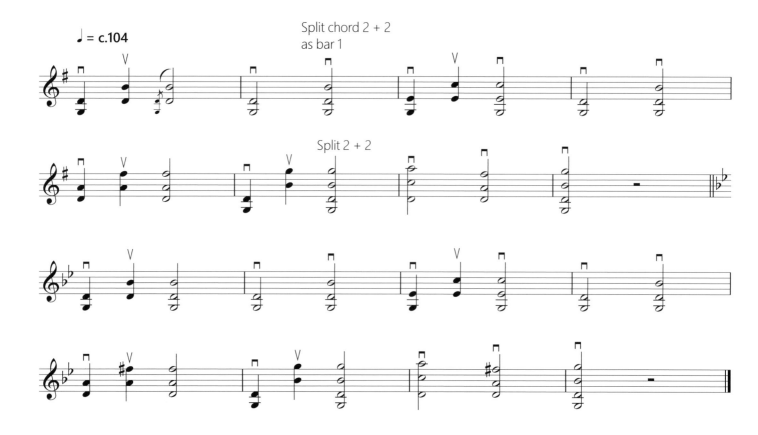

String crossings over 3 strings, with bowing variety Again, check the bow is at 90° to the string. For both bowing styles, use just enough bow and aim for evenness, particularly in the third and fourth notes of each bar. The saltando needs a very light bow hold and a little kick-start to the first note to activate the springing staccato – then just let the bow do most of the work. (Try on open strings only, for a couple of bars.)

1. legato ♩. = **c.132**
2. saltando ♩. = **c.192**

String crossings over 4 strings, with bowing variety This time, in the saltando version, the initial kick-start has to get the bow across four strings. To maintain tone quality and control, be careful to use just enough bow travel. It helps to be in a bow lane nearer to the fingerboard than usual.

1. legato ♩. = **c.132**
2. saltando ♩. = **c.192**

Baroque-style sequence At each change of key, listen carefully to the first finger, which needs to move in a wide semitone, as in a chromatic scale. The leading-note semitones, for example, C♯ to D in the first bar, need to be tighter.

Tech-Synthesis 2

Set 3

Much of this set is about finding 'just the right amount' of energy, stretch, accuracy and evenness. It's important to work step by step – don't try to achieve everything in one go. Work from the known to the almost known and allow information to settle.

- ❖ Golden Tone 3: in harmonics
- ❖ Judging bow energy in one-octave and two-octave harmonics
- ❖ Gradually increasing intervals between 1st and 4th fingers
- ❖ Chromatic fingering pattern option one
- ❖ Accuracy of finger placement in fourths and octaves
- ❖ Evenness in repeated finger action
- ❖ Evenness and note length accuracy in fast triplets
- ❖ Tech-Synthesis 3

Practising is a way of feeding your brain, which will take in whatever you give it – so allow all negative and overly self-critical thoughts to drift away. (And no chasing after them, either.)

Golden Tone exercise in one-octave harmonics 1 Use a bow lane that
works well on your violin for harmonics. It's interesting placing a harmonic
in a slur after an open string. Once the harmonic is started, check how much
bow travel and bow speed is needed to keep it clear and even.

Golden Tone exercise in one-octave harmonics 2 Starting a harmonic
from silence is harder, as it requires a kick-start from a bow which is already
on the string, followed by calm, balanced bow travel. Land the bow silently
before playing each new harmonic and remember that the kick-start, weight,
and speed of bow travel will be different for each string.

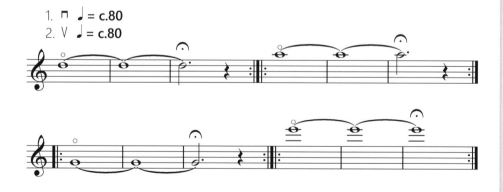

Now tune violin, as normal

Quick changes of position and judging bow-stroke energy The harmonic notes
need a faster, lighter bow. It's important to stay absolutely focussed, at the same time
thinking ahead to re-balance the bow speed and weight. Also take care with the open
strings, so they don't sound too loud.

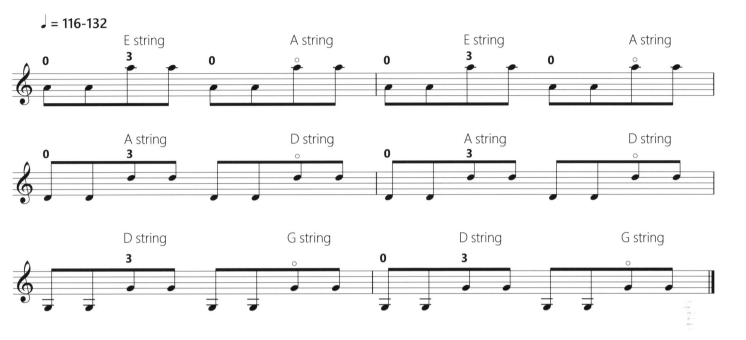

Two-octave harmonics No position changes here, but it's not always easy to get the
fingers on the exact spot for the diamond-shaped harmonics. Diamond harmonics need
a special kick-start, so every bow stroke needs careful preparation and anticipation.

1st finger to 4th finger, the interval increasing by semitones An exercise where it's important to listen for a rising chromatic pattern in the top notes, anticipating all the sounds in your head. I love the slight feeling of risk in these shifts and the thrill of getting all the 4th fingers spot on!

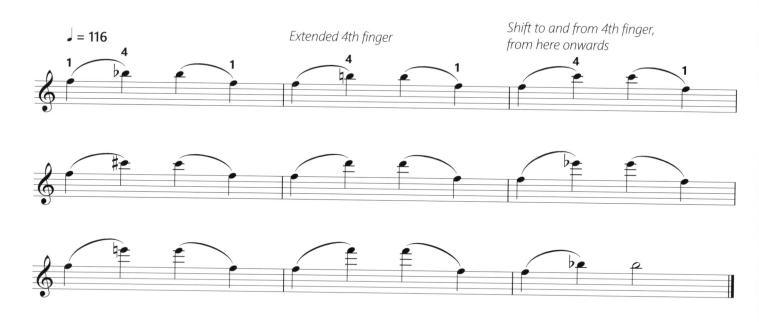

Chromatic passage fingerings 1 Bar 1 gives a sense of the space to be filled by these wide chromatic semitones. On each string, listen carefully, checking that all the lowest and highest ♫ match the tuning of the ♩s.

Perfect fourths This is one of the harder intervals to imagine accurately in your head. Here the lower note of the double stop is introduced in a musical phrase, making the interval easier to pitch. Play confidently, listening to the resultant tones in the double stops.

Fourths and octaves This sequence is about placing, re-placing, and moving the third finger – it needs concentration and accuracy to place it on the upper string so it doesn't catch the open string. Always listen for intonation to match each time the notes come round again.

Four exercises to develop evenness in repeated finger action When working towards complete finger control, start with very slow playing and only try a faster tempo when all the notes are absolutely even at ♩ = 72. Remember to feel a lift-off as well as a dropping action in the fingers, and keep the fingers down wherever possible, without creating unnecessary tension.

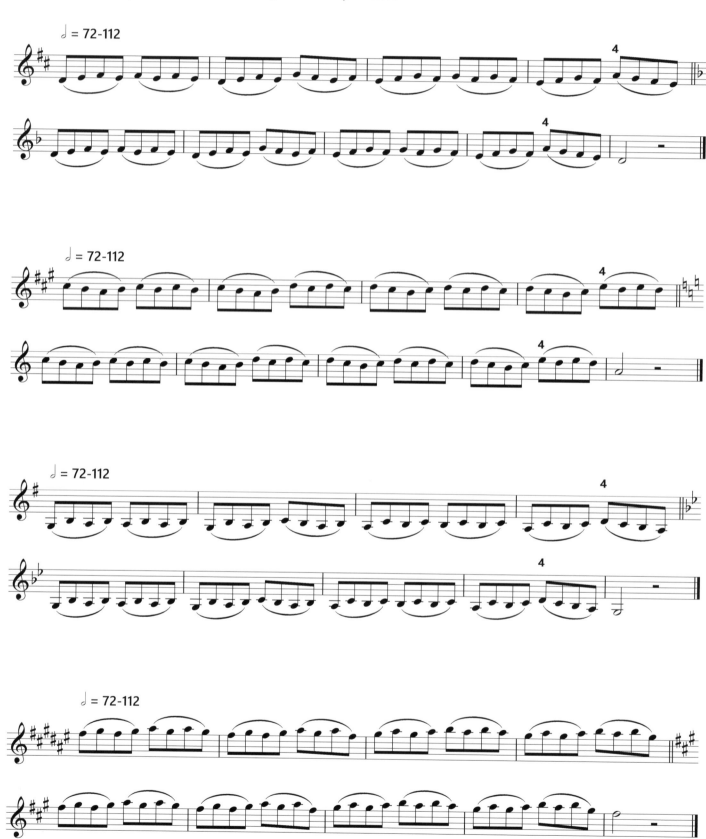

Developing evenness in triplets Keeping to an exact pulse in triplet passages can often be hard. So here each bar ends with a full beat, giving the chance to 're-run' the previous six notes in your head. This helps to keep the pulse and also to prepare for the next group of triplets. For variety, practise this either a bow to a beat, or a bow to a bar.

Tech-Synthesis 3

Notes

Set 4

Working at the accuracy of thirds, sixths and octaves in first position
helps to keep intonation in good health – a kind of super-food for your
violin playing.

❖ Golden Tone 4: with a change of string

❖ Preparing double stopping in thirds, sixths and octaves

❖ Working with awkward scale fingerings

❖ Martelé and spiccato

❖ Rising sequence on the lower strings

❖ Tech-Synthesis 4

Reliable intonation sometimes
depends on establishing
foundations that may at first
seem strangely counter-intuitive.

Golden Tone 4

The new element here is changing string and bow direction smoothly, at extreme ends of the bow, with minimal break in sound. Think ahead as these changes approach, getting ready to adjust the right arm smoothly. On the lower strings, it's important not to raise the right shoulder more than necessary.

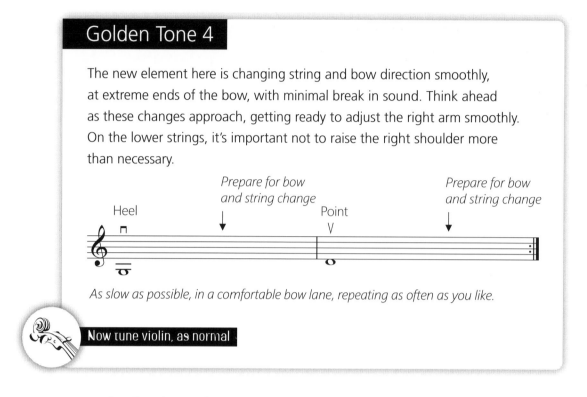

As slow as possible, in a comfortable bow lane, repeating as often as you like.

Now tune violin, as normal

Intervals of major and minor thirds as chords Here in the double stopping, the minor thirds played with 1st and 3rd fingers need a wider stretch than the major thirds. And against the open string, the 2nd finger needs to be high in the minor third and low in the major third.

Combining thirds, sixths and octaves 1 In the ♪s use just enough bow, combined with just enough arm movement. For variety, sometimes start with an Ⅴ.

Combining thirds, sixths and octaves 2 The same exercise transposed, so now there are no open strings! Keep fingers down wherever helpful, and try the bars of ♩s without vibrato, then with vibrato.

Different ways of fingering scale passages Sometimes in the middle of a piece
a disaster happens and you can find yourself playing a passage in the wrong position,
battling with an uncomfortable fingering. To deal with that situation, it's useful to train
the 'autopilot' to store alternative (awkward) scale fingerings, which don't lie so easily
under the hand.

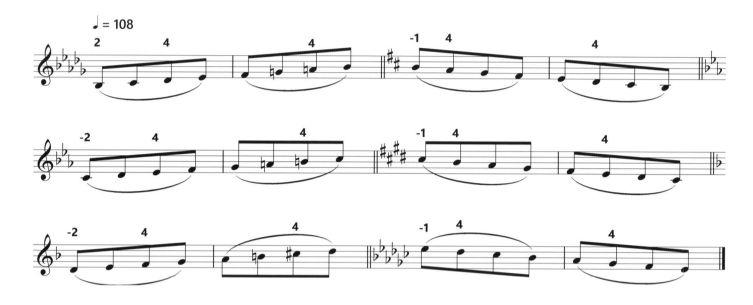

Jumping strings in martelé (in first position throughout) Martelé is often used
in string crossings, especially in 18th-century repertoire. There's a lot to think about in
this exciting and energetic style. Each bow stroke needs a short, sharp accent followed
by an immediate release of pressure, allowing the bow to travel before being reloaded
for the next accent. To cross over the strings silently in the tenths, stop all the energy,
but keep the bow in contact with a string at all times.

Lower strings sequence To help with accuracy of intonation, keep checking that the left hand is high enough above the fingerboard to enable fingers to work freely and comfortably. Sequences like this are enjoyable to play with lots of energy and rising dynamics, as in a Baroque piece.

Spiccato in even groups Another great bowing style. Use a tiny amount of bow, listening for evenness of note length and dynamic level, especially when changing string. Play the open strings as marked, taking care not to let them sound louder than the fingered notes.

♩ = 144

1. *p* light spiccato
2. *mf* heavier spiccato, slightly nearer to the heel

Spiccato in groups of three To work at the evenness of spiccato passages in groups of three, practise first with light accents on the first of each group. This is to establish in the brain the sense of each group beginning with a different bow direction. Then play it again without accents, just thinking about where they were.

1. Light accents
2. No accents

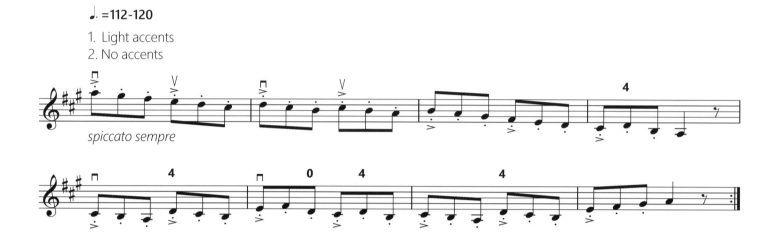

spiccato sempre

Tech-Synthesis 4

Set 5

A real work-out for intonation in a variety of situations – and a pizzicato marathon. But remember, when things get challenging, mistakes and imperfections can help to nourish the learning process.

- ❖ Golden Tone 5: in a rising chromatic pattern, Sul G

- ❖ Finger substitution

- ❖ Ascending passage work in high positions, across the A and E strings and across the D and A strings

- ❖ Scales as passage work

- ❖ Preparation for fingered chromatic scales

- ❖ A challenging shift sequence

- ❖ Pizzicato passage work

- ❖ Tech-Synthesis 5

If you notice that something is wrong, take a breath, relax, and think through what it was, and how you might try this or that differently, as an experiment.

Golden Tone 5

Golden Tone exercise in a slow chromatic pattern 1 Play *mf* really close to the bridge but not absolutely against it. Use just enough bow speed, travel and weight to get a mixture of overtones and pitch. This chromatic pattern, repeated on the other 3 strings is an excellent exercise for 'opening up' an instrument after it's had some repair work, or a new bridge, or set of strings.

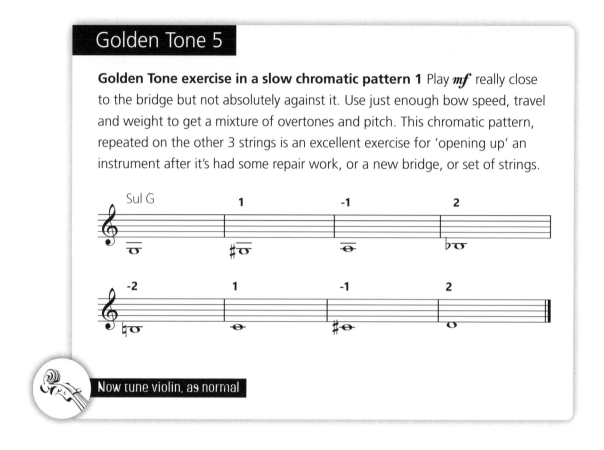

Now tune violin, as normal

Finger substitution in position changing This technique can provide the solution to fingering an awkward moment in passage work. Try it in a range of tempi and dynamics.

A higher passage-work sequence As the left hand starts to go round the shoulder in the position changes, check the left elbow adjusts to the best place for fingers to reach the fingerboard comfortably. And as the hand contracts, listen really carefully to the tuning, especially the semitones. (You may like to continue the sequence.)

Scales as passage work This is fun to play fast but for secure intonation begin by working at it slowly, especially the bars with awkward string crossings! To keep your brain alert, try varying your use of open strings and 4th fingers.

Stay in first position throughout

Ascending sequence, on the middle strings For a comfortable and smooth transition from 3rd position to 5th position on the middle strings, it's important to start with the left elbow high enough to enable the fingers to reach the fingerboard comfortably. The elbow and hand position need to adjust at each key change.

Chromatic fingerings 2 Resist the temptation to just take a run at chromatic scales and play this slowly the first time, to really focus on accuracy and clean shifts. (Remember to use wide, 'tempered tuning', semitones.) Create some phrasing and dynamics in the repeat.

A challenging shift sequence This is quite a tricky pattern to get into your head.
As well as listening to the tuning, remember to release the thumb to 'harmonic
pressure' during the shifts, so it can glide effortlessly.

1. Without vibrato, in a comfortable tempo
2. Slowly, with vibrato, in a Romantic style (think Brahms, or Fauré, perhaps)

*Adjust
elbow*

Fingering as above

Sixteen notes in first position, in a range of key signatures It's amazing
how much concentration this simple-looking exercise requires. Practise slowly first,
for intonation, then as fast as you can while still maintaining accuracy! The left-hand
pizzicato at the end of each line needs to be 'placed' with a clear sound, in strict tempo.

Pizzicato passage work Extended sections in pizzicato can come as a shock!
So this is a work-out for evenness of tone production across the strings, and in
different positions, which it's useful to practise in a wide variety of tempi and
dynamics. Sometimes we have to play pizzicato passages while holding the bow,
sometimes we can put the bow down, and occasionally we are asked to play
'banjo-style'. Good to be prepared for all these situations!

Stay in 2nd position

Tech-Synthesis 5

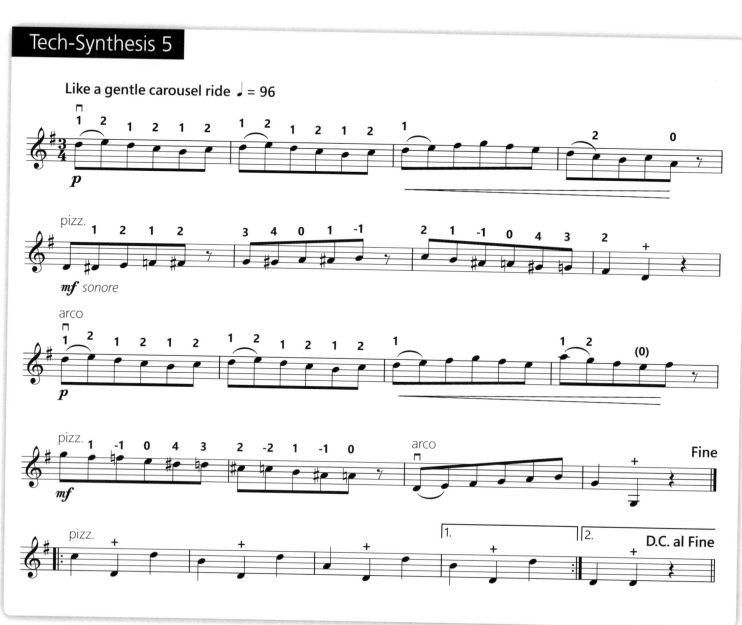

Set 6

Extending and developing shifting skills, intonation in passage work
and fast bowing at the extreme ends of the bow. It's easy at this stage
to start playing in autopilot – especially if this is a warm-up. Be careful
to stay alert, listen intently, and notice how your body is adjusting
during rotation and position changes.

- ❖ Golden Tone 6: in a rising chromatic pattern, Sul D
- ❖ Working at silent 'ghost' notes in shifts
- ❖ A variety of one-octave scales on the E string
- ❖ Arpeggios and sevenths in passage work
- ❖ Safe development of stretches
- ❖ Moving position downwards or upwards, by extension
- ❖ Introducing playing in two parts
- ❖ Fast ♪s in legato, at the heel and the point
- ❖ Tech-Synthesis 6

If it's an experiment, it's an experiment – you can always learn something from it. If something becomes worse because of an experiment, try the opposite instead.

Golden Tone 6

Golden Tone exercise in a slow chromatic pattern 2 Unusually, this version is in a normal lane. Try using a light vibrato.

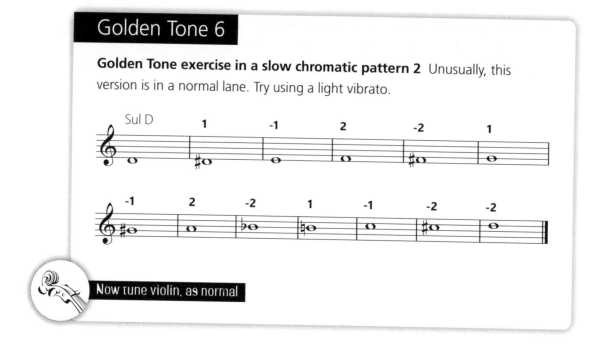

Now tune violin, as normal

Slow shifting with silent 'ghost' 1st fingers From bar 2, the shaded note marks the 'ghost' 1st finger D. It's important to have this accurate silent finger established in autopilot, to relate intervals to.

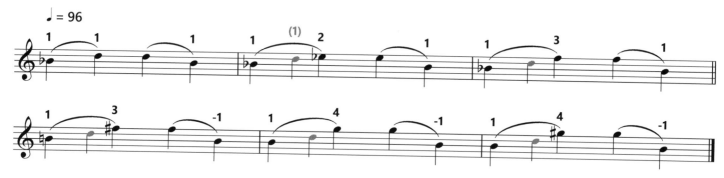

Faster shifting major key exercise with silent 'ghost' 1st fingers The ghost note here is A. (Also try transposing to the A string, adjusting the rotation of the left hand and elbow.)

Faster shifting minor key exercise, with silent 'ghost' 1st fingers The ghost note here is G. (Also try transposing to the G string, adjusting the rotation of the left hand and elbow.)

One-octave scales on a single string It's useful to work at this in a wide variety
of tempi and in various challenging combinations of slurred and separate bowings.
Try swapping the bowings around in the different keys.

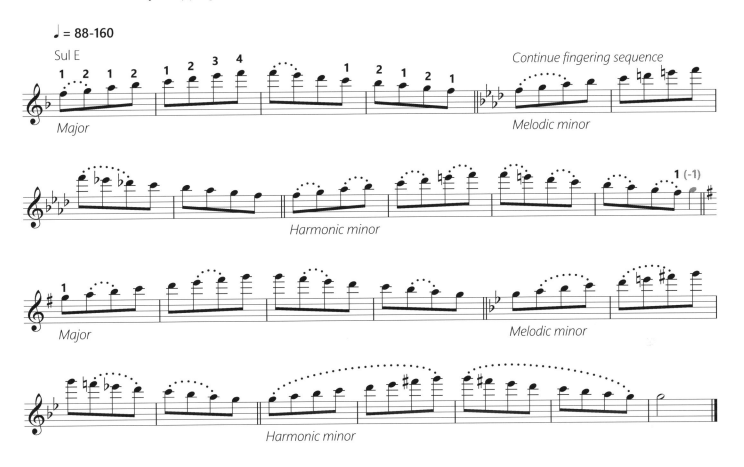

One-octave arpeggios and sevenths across two strings Another exercise
to practise in different tempi and with a variety of slurred and separate bowings
(as above). It helps to imagine the intervals in your head.

Developing stretches safely 1 Wisely, I was taught to stretch from the highest note towards the lowest and NEVER from the lowest to the highest, as that could strain the hand. I would add: don't over-practice stretches, and stop straight away if it ever feels really uncomfortable!

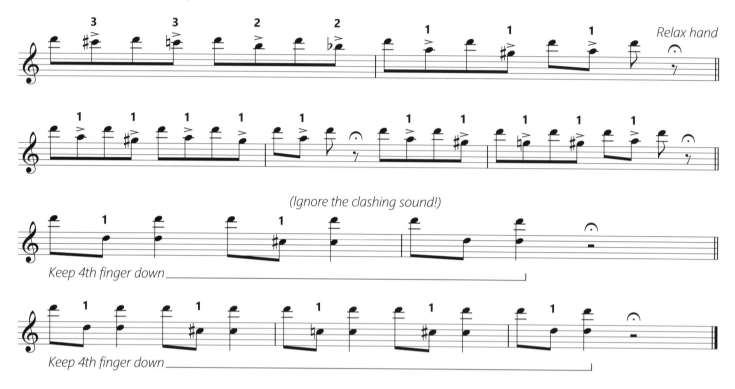

(Ignore the clashing sound!)

Keep 4th finger down

Keep 4th finger down

Moving position downwards, by extension A really useful fingering technique, particularly in Baroque and early Classical pieces. (I think of it as 'crawling' rather than 'shifting'.) Remember to keep adjusting your elbow.

Moving position upwards, by extension Another useful fingering solution.

Playing in two parts 1 In passages like this, check left-hand finger angles and left elbow position, and balance the bow weight so both lines come out clearly.

1. Without vibrato, in a comfortable tempo ♩ = **c.60**
2. Faster, perhaps in a dramatic Russian or Hungarian style!

Fast legato playing at the heel and point I love the confidence that this exercise brings! It's excellent for bow control. Prepare by lifting and landing silently at the heel and point a few times.

1. ♩ = **100**
2. ♩ = **132**
3. ♩ = **144**

Right by the heel   *Almost to the point*   *Back to the heel*

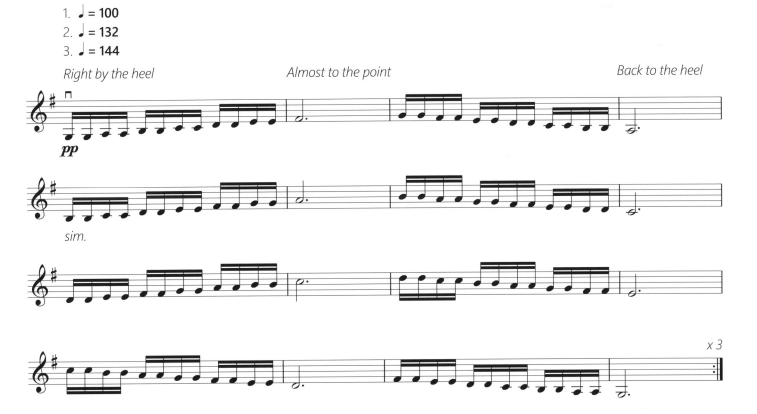

Playing in two parts 2 This transposed exercise is harder now as there are
no open strings! Take care adjusting the hand between each set of strings.

Tech-Synthesis 6

Misterioso ♩ = 116
Right at the heel

Set 7

It's important to maintain breath control when playing – sometimes we can become so engrossed we forget to breathe at all! This set provides opportunities for thinking about your own breathing and the 'breathing of the bow'. Calm focus, combined with controlled energy, is essential for both the left hand and right hand as technique is stretched and developed here.

❖ Golden Tone 7: double stopping

❖ Artificial harmonics

❖ Shifts with varied fingerings

❖ Developing playing in two parts

❖ Using a 'ghost' finger in descending shifts

❖ Developing wider stretches safely

❖ Sequences of shifts

❖ String crossing with bowing variations

❖ Spiccato, ricochet and portato

❖ Fourth finger work-out

❖ Tech-Synthesis 7

'Where you are'
is where you are
for the moment.

Golden Tone 7

First, tune violin

Golden Tone exercise in double stopping Place the bow between the bridge and fingerboard. This exercise is based on what we do when tuning our strings in fifths, when we listen for the production of 'resultant tones' (a form of harmonics). Move the bow at a speed that produces a constant strong sound, to encourage the start of the resultant tones. Keep going, bowing freely, for as long as you like before changing strings. After a while, the resultant tones get stronger and themselves set off more resultant tones, producing an effect reminiscent of Tibetan ringing bowls.

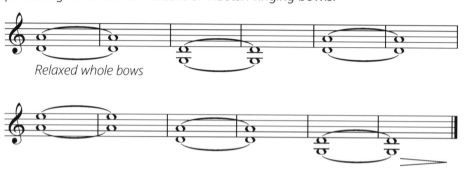

Relaxed whole bows

Artificial ('stopped') harmonics These are played with the 1st finger using normal pressure, while the 4th finger just rests on the string, as it would for a harmonic.

Artificial harmonics in shifts During the shifts the 1st finger has to go from normal pressure to harmonic pressure and back, while the 4th finger always uses harmonic pressure.

A sequence of shifts with varied fingerings Listen for the top notes of each section sounding exactly the same each time.

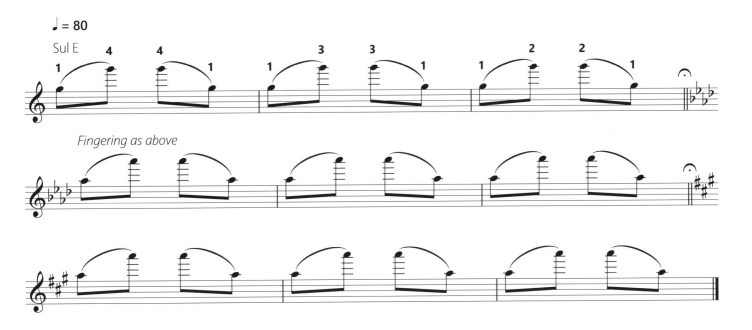

More playing in two parts The first two bars are a preparation for what will become the lower of the two parts. In the double stopping, balance the bow weight so the melody line is always heard clearly.

Using a 'ghost' finger in descending shifts A really useful fingering, when everything needs to be on one string and really 'clean'. As always, practice this slowly first, to develop accuracy. Listen for wide chromatic semitones at the changes of key, and the tighter semitones elsewhere. At the end of lines 3 and 4, the position change requires finger substitution.

Developing stretches safely 2 Here the stretch extends into a full tenth, so only work at this if you are feeling warmed up. For small hands, it's definitely not suitable for the first day back after a break! Listen for wide chromatic semitones in the descending first fingers. *(See also **Developing stretches safely 1**, page 46.)*

Sequences of shifts It's useful to work at shifting in exercises within a key, as it's not an exact sequence of intervals. Try this slowly first, to check that shifting technique and intonation are staying 'clean' across all four strings, then enjoy the faster tempo!

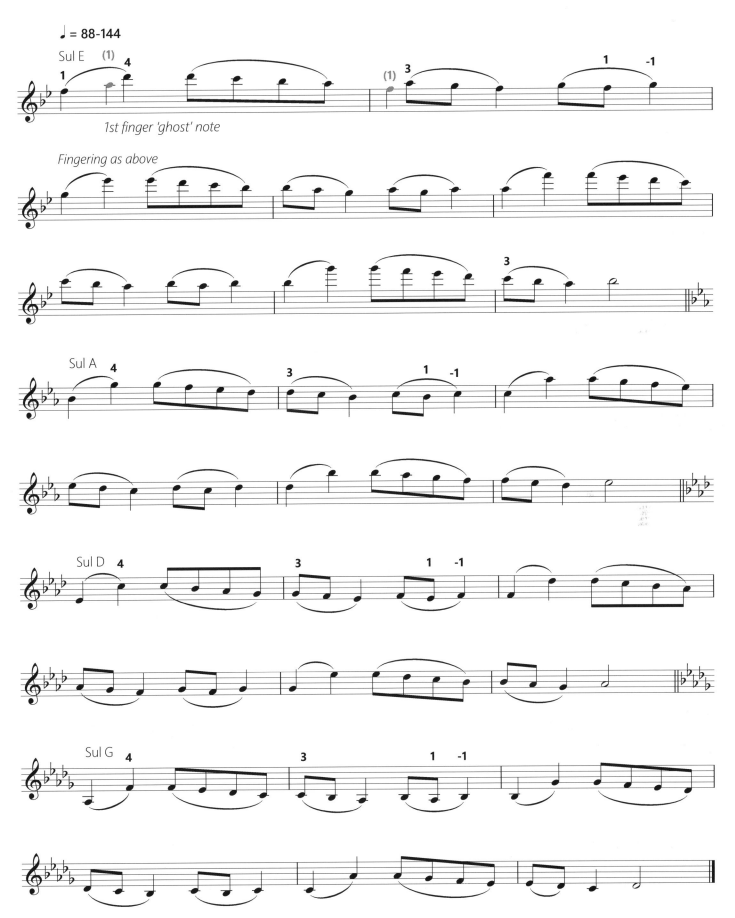

1st finger 'ghost' note

Fingering as above

String crossing exercise, with four variations in different bowing styles

It's good to know which part of your bow is best for these bow strokes at different
dynamic levels. When you try the different articulation suggestions, notice how much
the bow travel needs to adjust.

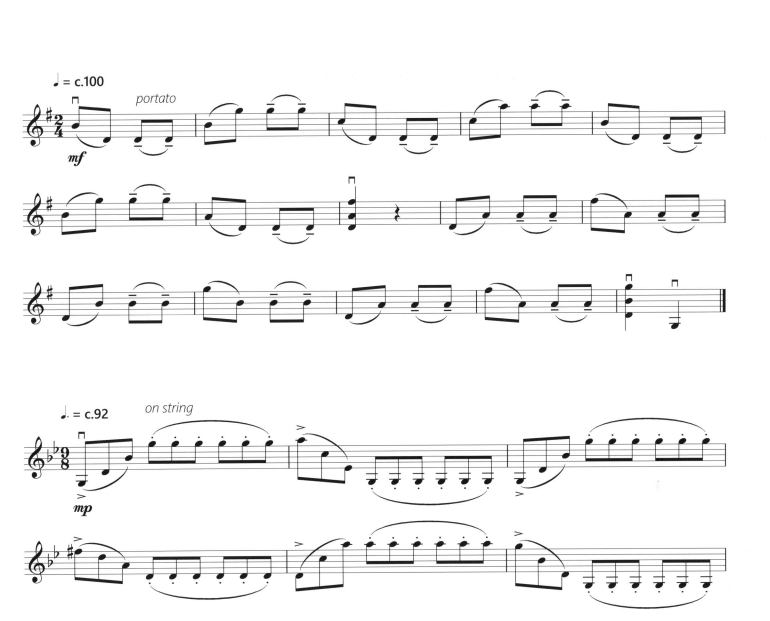

♩ = c.80

1. **mp** spiccato
2. **f** spiccato

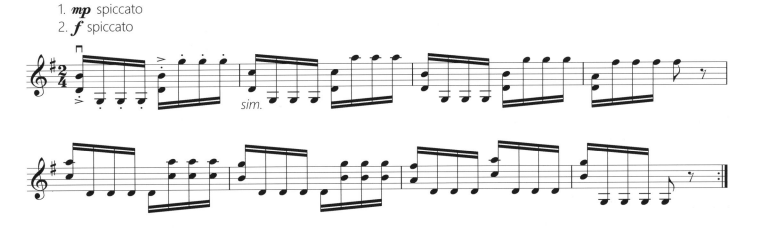

Fourth finger work-out Try starting either V or ⊓ and alternate the slur options between the strings.

1. ♩ = 80
2. ♩ = 132

Take a moment

Tech-Synthesis 7

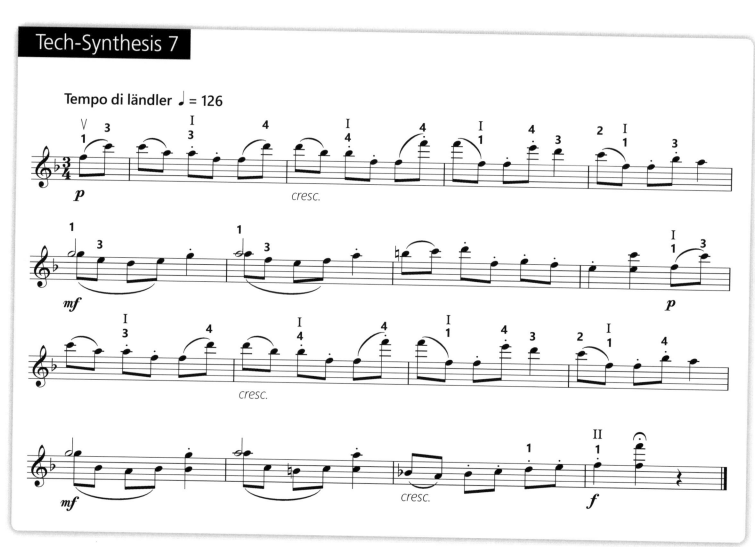

Tempo di ländler ♩ = 126

Set 8

Key skills developed in this set are the anticipation of sounds in your head and intense listening. Harmonics and tremolo offer extra colour.

❖ Golden Tone 8: as a one-octave minor scale, Sul G

❖ Matching intonation when playing the same notes with alternative fingerings in different positions

❖ Sequences, shifting by extension

❖ Shifting in sixths and fifths

❖ Dramatic 'final note' harmonics

❖ Double stopping in a chromatic sequence

❖ Tech-Synthesis 8

> If something goes well, 'step back' and enjoy the moment. Feel good about yourself.

Golden Tone 8

**Golden Tone exercise as a one-octave natural minor scale on the
G string** Place the bow really close to the bridge, producing just enough
defined pitch to hear that it's a scale. Start with weightless balance, then
find a left elbow position which allows fingers to drop onto the fingerboard
easily and comfortably. Just before each shift, think ahead: adjust the height of
the left elbow and hand, to negotiate the moves to fifth and seventh positions
smoothly, without disturbing the bow. (And remember to keep breathing!)

Now tune violin, as normal

Matching intonation: playing the same notes in different positions It takes
focussed concentration to get an exact match for all three bars. Use a steady tempo
and keep the harmony flowing.

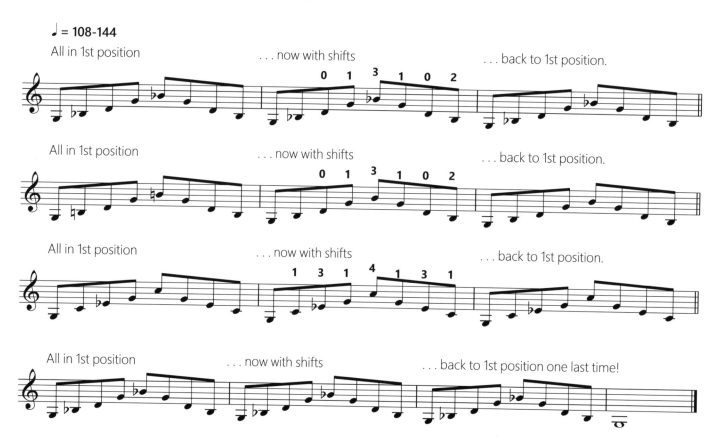

Matching intonation, using alternative chromatic fingerings Tempo and
musical context always influence the choice of chromatic fingerings. This exercise
uses both versions twice, to help maintain equal fluency in both options.

♩ = c.138

1. Separate bows
2. One bow to a bar

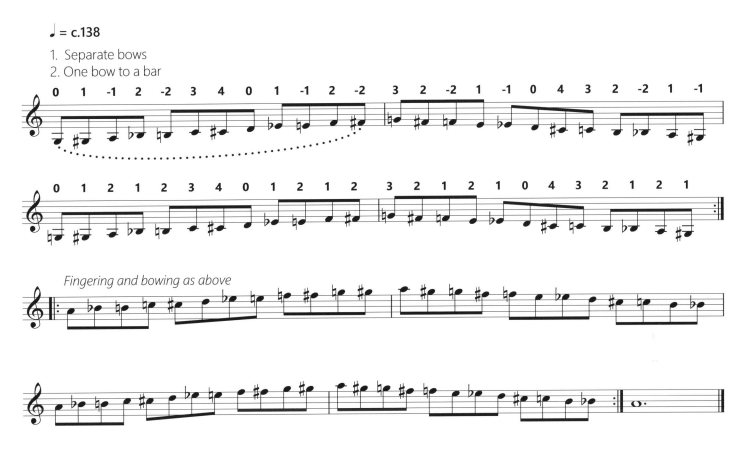

Fingering and bowing as above

More shifting by extension Look out for semitones and listen carefully to the
melodic line created by the first ♪ in each group.

♩. = c.80

Shifting in sixths and fifths Give this an element of phrasing by thinking of the last note of each group of ♩♪♪♪ as an upbeat. Listen for the melodic lines created by all the lower notes and all the upper notes.

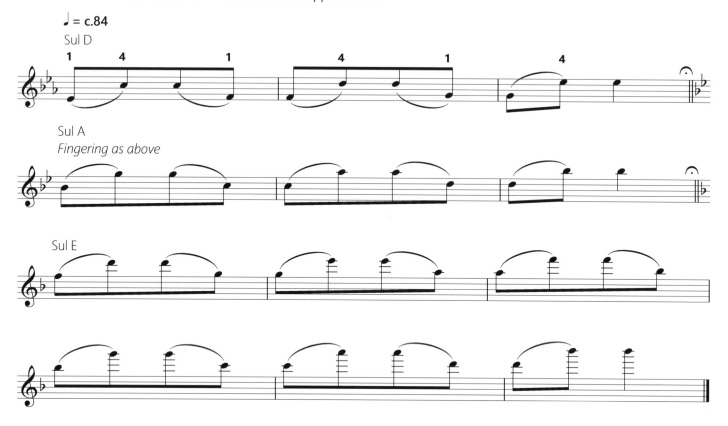

Dramatic harmonics! It's really worth spending time on this special technique for getting harmonics to zing out! With total focus and coordination, kick-start the harmonic and play the normal note value. At the end of the note, lift the finger and bow off the string simultaneously, with energy. As the bow leaves the string, make a curved follow-through.

Tremolo without tension Starting in weightless balance, place the bow near the point. Think of the string supporting your bow and you will be able to control it with hardly any pressure – so no gripping and no tension required. Kick-start the tremolo with one tiny, fast ⊓. Then to keep it going, imagine that your bow arm, from the knuckles to the elbow, is a kind of see-saw. Let this see-saw rise and fall alternately a tiny amount, with as little active intervention as possible. Stop if you feel any tension. Take a moment or so, then try again. This relaxed feeling works in ♪ passages too. *(See **Tech-Synthesis 8**, page 63.)*

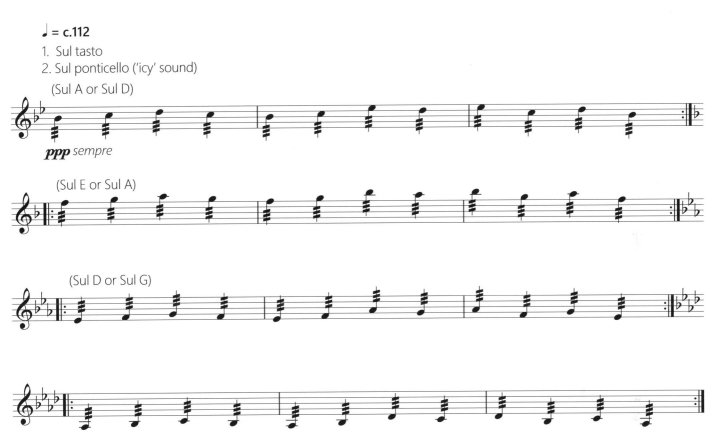

Shifting in octaves and sevenths Again, give this some phrasing by thinking of the last note of each group of ♫ ♫ as an upbeat. Shifting always feels better when given some musical context.

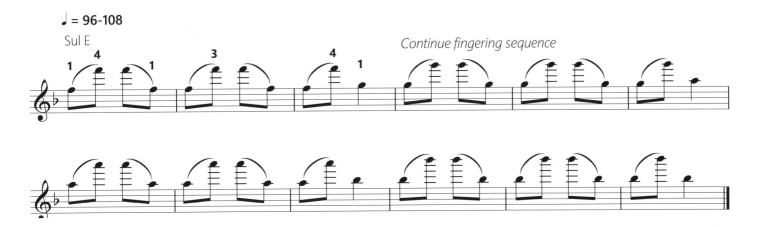

A descending sequence in the descending melodic minor We spend a lot of time working at contracting the hand as we go into higher positions, so it's good to work at the opposite skill.

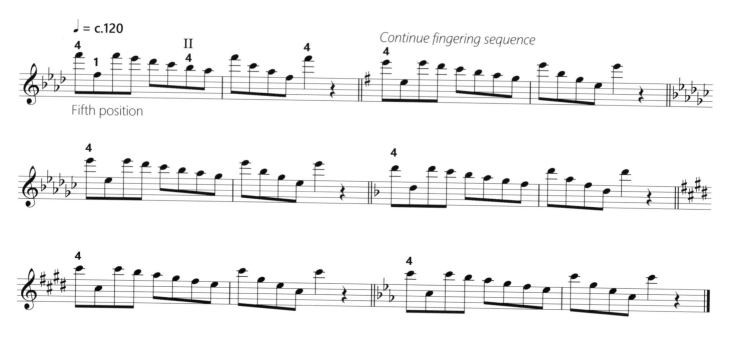

Fifth position

Double-stopping octaves in a chromatic sequence Listen carefully to the semitones at the changes of position, checking that they are wide enough.

Matching intonation in passages of diminished 7th patterns It's useful to be fluent
at alternative fingerings for these intervals, ready for awkward passage work!

Tech-Synthesis 8

Notes

Set 9

Total immersion in the whole-tone sound world is combined in this set with intensive work at finger control and further development of double stopping.

❖ Golden Tone 9: as a whole-tone scale

❖ Whole-tone patterns and phrases

❖ Shifting by extension in whole tones

❖ Double stopping within whole-tone phrases

❖ Fourths, fifths and sixths in double stopping

❖ Extreme slow finger control

❖ Fast finger control

❖ Tech-Synthesis 9

Always look for the simplest effective route.

Golden Tone 9

Golden Tone exercise as a whole tone scale Use just enough bow weight and travel to get a consistent, ethereal **_pp_**. Try 'imagining' the sound of each note before playing it.

Sul A

Now tune violin, as normal

Patterns in consecutive whole tones Play gently, perhaps thinking of a moonlit scene. In the repeat, try imagining the sound of each phrase before playing it. The first four-note phrase should sound familiar – a progression like this is to be found starting on the second ♪ of the third bar on page 12. Pencil in any helpful enharmonic equivalents and try the bracketed fingerings in the repeat.

♩ = c.100

Answering phrases in whole tones This time the slurred staccatos add some lightness to the texture. As before, pencil in any helpful enharmonic equivalents and in the repeat, try imagining each phrase before playing it.

♩ = c.88

1. **_mf_** 2. **_p_**

Crawling shifts in whole tones If you're not used to whole tone scales, the chromatic notation can make it look much harder than it is! At first you might find it helpful to 'translate' some of the notes enharmonically and pencil in these alternatives. For example, if the first two notes were written as F♯ and A♯ you would probably be able to imagine a major third.

A simple whole tone exercise with double stopping Although at first glance this might look complicated, each bar has the same combination of intervals. Aurally the first four quavers sound like consecutive major thirds, and the double stop sounds like a minor sixth. (Again, pencil in enharmonic alternatives if it helps.)

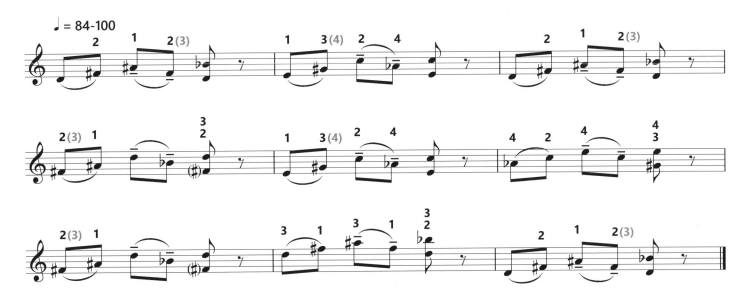

Perfect fifths in double stopping in first position The position of the left elbow, and the height and angle of the fingers, is crucial for the tuning of fifths – and these need to adjust for each combination of strings. Notice how the finger pads need to contact the fingerboard slightly differently from usual to get accurate intonation when double stopping the fifths. (And if you have to play on a different instrument, there is always a slight adjustment needed to find where the fifths are.)

Slow finger control using the Dorian mode Start with weightless balance and concentrate with stress-free focus. Let one finger at a time drop from as high as possible, then lift upwards back to this starting height, with an exaggerated spring. Continue this way for the whole exercise, staying in the zone, and not thinking about getting to the end! This kind of detailed attention to finger action is often used by virtuoso players to 'deep clean' their technique.

Perfect fifths and major sixths Listen for matching intonation in the single-note intervals of sixths and the double-stopped sixths. You may have to adjust the angle of the finger pads to achieve this.

♩ = c.104

non vib.

Developing fast finger control using the Phrygian mode Use the 'dropping' and 'springing' action from the slow finger control exercise. It takes even more control to get the exaggerated active lift-off in this fast version! (Try this with a metronome.)

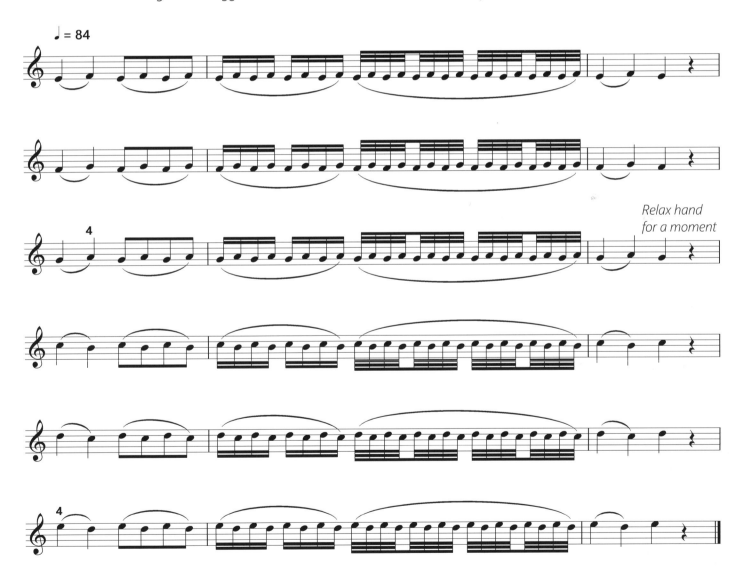

♩ = 84

Relax hand for a moment

Perfect fourths, perfect fifths and minor sixths As always, listen for matching intonation, and adjust finger angles. Enjoy playing the repeated ⊓ chords in *grandioso* style.

Tech-Synthesis 9

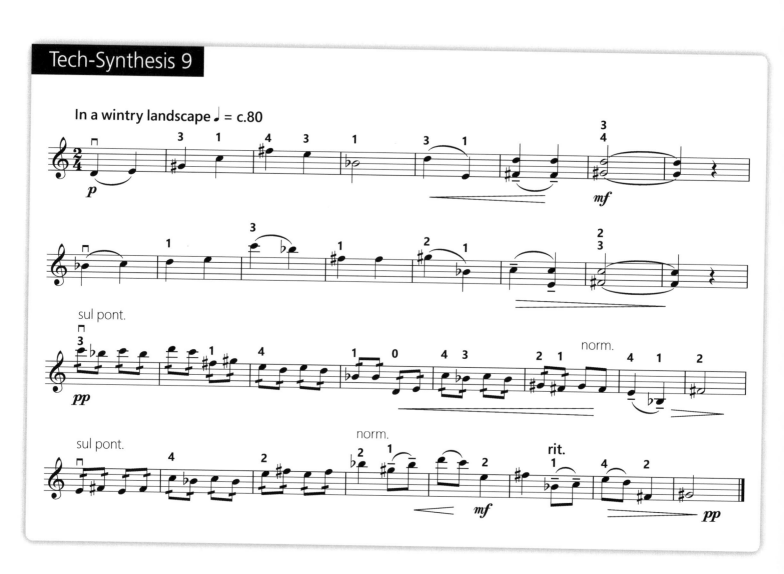

Set 10

This set has left-hand and right-hand techniques to support 'showy' violin repertoire. And with a flourish, the final Tech-Synthesis pulls together skills from all the sets.

- ❖ Golden Tone 10
- ❖ 24 notes to a bow
- ❖ Slurs and slurred staccato
- ❖ Double stopping in contracting intervals
- ❖ Thirds in sequences
- ❖ Shifting with sevenths and octaves, and with ninths and octaves
- ❖ A strategy for accuracy in fast playing across all the strings
- ❖ Energising chords
- ❖ Tech-Synthesis 10

Music making is a journey. Sometimes we need to step sideways for a while but we can always return and continue the journey later.

Golden Tone 10

The almost silent Golden Tone exercise Play with the bow tilted, close to the fingerboard, using just a few hairs. Concentrating on keeping the big toes in contact with the ground may have a surprising effect on how slowly you can bow.

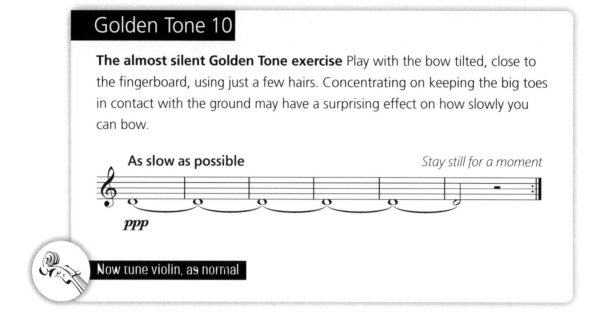

Now tune violin, as normal

Fast playing, with 24 notes to a bow The main focus here is managing the bow travel, so there's enough bow to finish each slur comfortably. Keep the angle of the bow as narrow as possible when moving between strings. There are some places where you could use either a 4th finger or an open string. Being equally good at both is useful but always decide ahead, to let your brain know which you want to do! As a challenge, try the repeat with 48 notes to a bow!

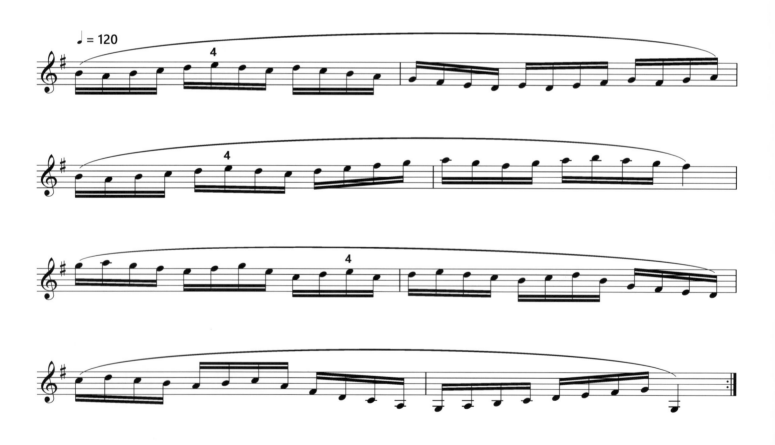

Slurs and slurred staccatos All of the ♪'s are of equal value, so this is an exercise in controlling bow travel, as the number of notes to a bow alternates between two and three. Enjoy giving the staccato notes distinctive lightness of character. Listen carefully to the first finger at the changes of position – sometimes the shift is a tone, sometimes a semitone.

Double stopping in contracting intervals For many violinists, double stopping the semitone of E♭ and D in first position is quite a stretch. It requires maximum rotation of the left arm and is especially difficult for a small hand. This exercise only arrives at that hard interval in the penultimate bar. Along the way, rotation and stretch are developed in stages, starting with the easier strings. At the start of each line, the elbow and arm position should be raising the hand high enough above the fingerboard for fingers to drop onto the lower string without any strain. As with tenths, do not try the hard semitone double-stops on the lower strings if you feel any pain, or if you haven't played for a while.

A sequence of major thirds The height of the left elbow needs to adjust to ensure the finger pads can always reach comfortably without catching on an open string.

Shifting with major sevenths and octaves Listen for close leading-note semitones between all the top ♪s, while the first finger sometimes moves a tone and sometimes a semitone.

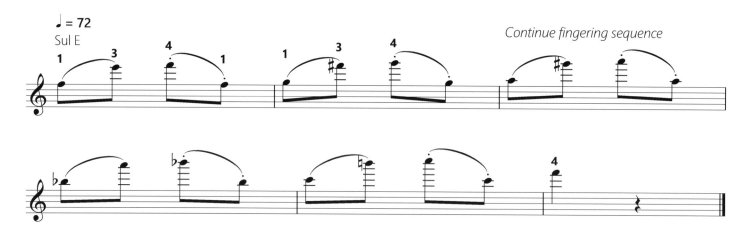

Shifting with ninths and octaves Here the first finger always moves by tones, while the top notes sometimes have an interval of a tone and sometimes a semitone.

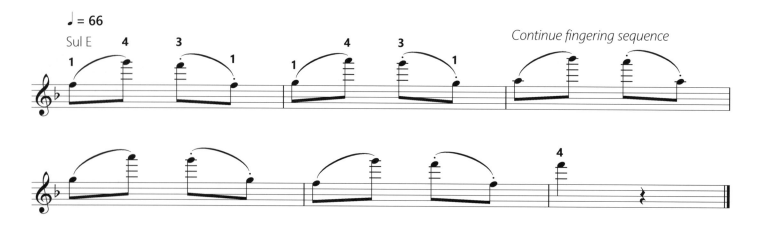

Fast playing across all the strings, in separate bows Before playing passages like this as written, my personal tactic is to play all the notes on all the correct strings without any fingers – as if it is all open strings (see cue-sized exercise below). This creates a kind of magnetic three-dimensional scaffolding, laying the foundation of the pattern of string crossings, making it easier for the brain to send the fingers and bow to the right places.

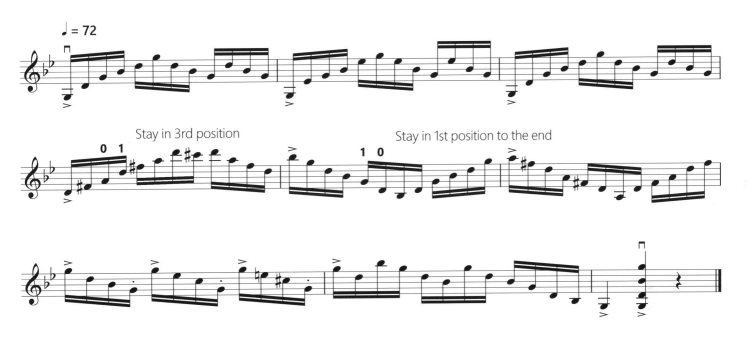

Here's the 3-D scaffolding for the piece above It's amazing how much of this string crossing looks counter-intuitive to begin with. It's also amazing how much practising time is saved if the brain has this scaffolding in place before working at the pitches.

A sequence of minor and major thirds Remember that the stretch between fingers is wider in the minor double stops. Keep the angle of the bow as narrow as possible in the slurred string crossings, as this will help the balance of the bow on the chords.

Continue fingering sequence

Energising chords An exciting chord happens when violin and bow come together with fast opposing energies, creating a sound which thrills through the instrument, the player's ears and the ears of anyone listening. My personal technique before each chord is to spend a millisecond 're-setting' weightless balance, then allow the violin to float upwards as the bow descends at speed in a curved action. (I also think of it as the violin 'exhaling' through the f-holes during the left arm upward motion, and somehow this helps the bow to breathe too.)

> **Think:** *weightless balance, violin 'floats' upwards as bow simultaneously descends with great energy.*

Tech-Synthesis 10

In the style of a chaconne ♩ = c.112

Notes

An emergency two-minute warm up

❖   Spend 15 seconds in weightless balance

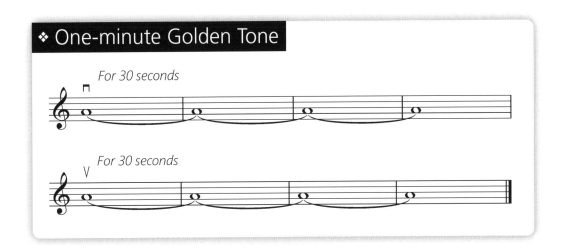

❖   Spend 15 seconds lifting and landing alternately at the heel and point

❖   Finish with this shifting exercise:

> **Challenge:** *To prepare for the eventuality of needing a silent emergency two-minute warm up, develop the ability to do the above sequence as quietly as possible!*

Also available by Mary Cohen:

BEGINNER

Superstart Violin and *Bags Of Fun For Violin* are ideal for developing basic skills, designed to be used simultaneously

GRADES 1–3

The *Superstudies Violin* series builds essential technical skills through fun and imaginative short pieces

GRADES 4–6

Technique Takes Off! Violin and *More Technique Takes Off! Violin* are complementary volumes, the second adopting a more modern approach

LATE INTERMEDIATE – ADVANCED

Technique Flies High! includes material in and out of the high positions, exploring a range of different sound worlds

Faber Music Limited, Burnt Mill, Elizabeth Way, Harlow, CM20 2HX
Tel: +44 (0) 1279 82 89 82 Fax: +44 (0) 1279 82 89 83
sales@fabermusic.com fabermusicstore.com